ON COURTING MARY AFTER EASTER

ON COURTING MARY AFTER EASTER

Poems

THOMAS RONALD VAUGHAN

RESOURCE *Publications* • Eugene, Oregon

ON COURTING MARY AFTER EASTER
Poems

Resource Publications
An Imprint of Wipf and Stock Publishers
199 W. 8th Ave., Suite 3
Eugene, OR 97401

www.wipfandstock.com

PAPERBACK ISBN: 979-8-3852-2555-2
HARDCOVER ISBN: 979-8-3852-2556-9
EBOOK ISBN: 979-8-3852-2557-6

06/27/24

Contents

JUS AD BELLUM: THE DEAD OF GAZA

I

If God, for Goodness sake, confers
The blessings that we need,
What is the attribution when
The hearts of nations bleed?

II

In *Lawrence of Arabia,* the far desert horizon bursts
Like popping bulbs from old cameras.
Omar Sharif says, "God bless the men under that."
Someone objects, "But they are our enemies, the Turks!"
Sharif replies, "God bless them anyway."

III

Did God command Israel to *genocide* Amalek,
Or did they do it and say He did?
One must be careful how one writes history:
God can read.

JUS AD BELLUM: theories of "Just War." *Lawrence of Arabi*a, 1961
motion picture.

HOMERE PATRIS PLESSY

Take a seat, Mr. Plessy, take a seat.
But seven-eights white will just not do.
This is Louisiana, and the Separate Car Act is Law Almighty.
You must tell the Conductor of your black Grandmother,
Then he will escort you to your proper place.
You cannot sit there, says both the Train and the State.
Take a stand, Mr. Plessy, take a stand.
Then off to the earth-shaking conclusion
Of "separate but equal," for Judge Ferguson says
Things are crystal clear and the State law does not
Violate any Amendment, as you claim.
Off again to the Supremes, and
Please sit down, Mr. Plessy, please sit down.
Highest yet, we proclaim that "separate but equal" it shall be,
And if the "Colored Race" chooses
To see the Fourteenth Amendment
As a badge of inferiority, it is their choice,
Not something inherent in the law itself.
So go home, Mr. Plessy, do go home.
Jim Crow is coming in spades,
Dancing both North and South, and though you will not
Live to see it, take heart, Mr. Plessy, pray take heart.
The Reverend Oliver Brown has strong educational demands
For his lovely children, and he will faithfully
Carry on, Mr. Plessy, carry on.
Then adieu, Mr. Plessy, fond adieu. Rest you well.

Homere Patris Plessy, 1862-1925. Rev. Oliver Leon Brown, 1918-1961. Plessy v. Ferguson, 1896, and Brown v. Board of Education, 1954, were landmark Supreme Court decisions in Civil Rights.

FLAVORS

I tasted every flavor in the room.
Her hair was dark, her eyes a China blue.
Before the walls of life came crashing down,
We talked of all the things that we would do.

I think of her with every passing day,
Though we are years and miles and miles apart.
Sad wonderment still has its sweet allure:
She tasted every flavor of my heart.

PROLOGUE TO A NOVEL ABOUT MARY AND JOSEPH

Since virtue was not at issue,
A maiden of the right circumstance had to be found.
Found, she struggled with the strange command.
No God, even her God, could replace the espoused's bed,
And who would believe such scandalous nonsense.
So, waiting in her agony for this Spirit,
Mary pondered those things in her heart.
It was her mistake at not knowing,
For the sickness began straightaway,
The pregnant nauseas of the unremembered union.
Joseph, in her cry, would not, could not
Be expected to countenance such events.
Confided in at last, he proved understanding,
But inwardly questioned the entire visitation.
Weeks passed, and Mary, too, in her reflection,
Was uncertain of the verbatim pronouncement,
Unclear as to exactly what had transpired and when.
But they were husband and wife now,
And even amid that tense and skeptical trust,
A child was coming into the world......

AN OWL WITH PLANTS

The owl sits in a flower vase,
An old crock too chipped for beans.
Above tower thin snake plants,
Twisting gently and slowly to sharp tips.
The earth which holds both is dark,
Clotted and fine, creeping up stalks
To indicate its one-time wetness.
The owl leans on a needle shaft of wood,
And peers off, with two glass eyes,
Into the eternity of this small room.

ANNIVERSARY

Was it *that* long ago
When we became "one,"
Like seeds blown into a wall,
Clinging to survive, bear roots, and thrive?
In those years roots have grown deep,
So profuse that we cannot tell
Plant from wall.
Whichever you are, I am the other.
Now that we are one, for this long,
We celebrate nothing alone.
There is no need to.

DROWNING IN RIP TIDE, SOUTH OF WILMINGTON

Where the road stops, the beach goes on
To where river meets Atlantic,
The place where undertow reigns.
I can swim there.
Impregnable, even if taken down,
I cannot drown,
My lungs are iron—
They need no air.
I breathe only because others do.
In this tide, there is no panic,
Only shared control,
Living with what moves.
If you breathe, you are lost,
But you need not breathe.
You can walk on sand,
Surveying the dark womb
That, if it could,
Would suck us back into itself.
For me, it will.
I volunteer.
Now, my limp arms float.
I am not flying.

HOPE

Hope springs eternal in the breast:
It does not spring in mine.
For I have tasted much of life,
And much of it is brine.

I sit under a leafy tree,
They will not be here long,
For Autumn winds are roaring in,
And Autumn winds are strong.

And so the seasons roll and change
As problems rise and fall,
But this one rips my heart in two,
And nothing helps at all.

THE POET LOSES ANOTHER GIRLFRIEND

Your photograph gives one good reason
Why she left- -you simply look like you don't fit in.
But this time, I think you will be devastated,
And discover at long last
That not even poetry
Can keep a relationship going.
And you thought everything turns
On the turn of a phrase.
Now you know how "ordinary" you are,
After all.

HATTIE McDANIEL

When Rhett Butler quite shockingly told Scarlett O'Hara,
"Frankly my dear, I don't give a damn,"
The audience gasped in jaw--dropping disbelief.
What concerned no one was the fact
That though Hattie McDaniel won an Oscar
For Best Supporting Actress,
She could not attend the Atlanta premiere,
And later had to sit at a "Segregated" table
During the whole glitzy, bubbly Award Show.
She died in 1952, and even then could not
Be buried in the all-- white Hollywood Cemetery.
Later, as others began to give a damn,
Situations grindingly changed.
In subsequent decades
Hattie's Statuette, lovingly given to Howard University,
Mysteriously disappeared, was relocated,
Then vanished, never to be seen again.

Hattie McDaniel (1893-1952), African-American actress and entertainer, played "Mammy" in *Gone with the Wind,* 1939 film.

FREUDIAN NEGOTIATIONS

My dear
I said
That we
Might wed
After I'd seen
Your Id
In bed.

Sigmund Freud (1856-1939), founder of psychoanalysis, used Id,
Ego, and Superego in his theories of the human psyche.

CONSCIENTIOUS OBJECTION

Good day, good night, which is it?
I cannot think to tell.
I am quite full of spirits,
And things do not look well.

I drank a toast to Goodness,
And to a friend I know,
And to the dozen others
Who left us long ago.

And when they mentioned valor
And going off to war,
I drained a full glass quickly
For I could do no more.

Since from the womb that bore me
I wear the armament
That Pacifism gave me,
I stand, and won't relent!

So rumored wars, eternal,
And friends go off to fight,
How sadly will I toast them
And argue with the night.

SHARPEVILLE

The Boer boys are looking for a gun
And must find it
Or hide one among the 69 dead bodies
Strewn before them on the patchy grass.
In the Beloved Country it has come to this,
And gone quite far enough.
Now, the powerless with no vote,
No rights, nothing,
Will do even better.
To be sure, lily white Dutch boys,
These blacks will find guns, ammunition,
And scarce flammables
For their most delicate Molotov bombs.
So do not wonder about weapons
On bullet-ridden corpses.
Your case cannot be made,
There is no defense,
And they are slowly coming for you
And every oppressive Apartheid thing
You have ever stood for.

On March 21, 1960, this massacre occurred at the Police Station in
Sharpeville, South Africa.
Cry, the Beloved Country, novel by Alan Patton (1903-1988), South
African writer.

THE FOURTH GOSPEL CHRIST

There was a man from John whose name was "Christ,"
Who told, at the drop of a hat,
That he was the Messiah sent from God.
Rather, see him as an agent,
Darting through lives,
Spying out the land and the lay of the mind,
Dropping secrets only to those
Who could make the miraculous transition in faith.
See him oblique, incognito, brash,
Throwing into rage who demanded,
"Are you the Christ? Tell me now!"
He would reply, "*You* say that I am."
And in that maddening, exquisite irony
The whole world froze.

HENRY V BEFORE AGINCOURT

These lines I write to thee, my Love, in haste.
The sun is rising and I must soon terminate this simple note.
I will pursue details in your arms
If ever I am home again.

Give prayers and blessing to my House.
Tell them their King has seen much
Of God's world, and has struck down in fury
A hundred English foes.

Should I perish in this present fight,
Say to them that I died
With sword in hand and prayer in heart.
Say that Christ and he held many a fierce enemy at bay.

Henry V (1386-1422). On St. Crispin's Day, 1415, though heavily
outnumbered, the English won a decisive victory over the French
at Agincourt.

GOODBYE, MY MOTHER

Goodbye, my mother.
I will not grieve you longer
As if some distant God took you away
And would not deal you back to me again,
As if your God in death were not my God in life:
She is.

Goodbye, my mother.
I will think of you when I read poems
Of the seasons change, of the farm,
And of those who succeeded
All the way to the destroying towns.
I will think of you as destroyed in this life only.

Goodbye, my mother.
I will seek you in a special way
When I am tempted to despair,
Individualizing it to my own powerlessness.
I will hear a word from you
Who triumphed in the face of worse, by far.

Goodbye, my mother.
This is Sunday in the Spring,
A day of beauty and of warmth.
It is Lent, a Passion leading to death,
A Resurrection to life again.
Even as I write, I will think of you as resurrected.

So goodbye, my mother.
It is inevitable that I memorialize,
And attach your meaning to things and words,
Places, gestures, and ideas.

In them, I will sense your presence, and make
Appropriate preparation for our eternal reunion.

LWB (1922-1993)

TIMES

"Things fall apart; the centre cannot hold …." W. B. Yeats

Forgotten now, for long since dead,
The march of peace addresses itself to nothing.
Decadence replaces honor.
Integrity, a thing to attribute
To times when life was liveable.
Haunting fears now hang
Where delicate dreams once attached,
Immovable, until the specter fell.
Deplorable people of premeditated pain
Unloose themselves on those who do not understand,
And ruthlessly crush from them
The last vapor of that which poisons hatred.
Amid these scenes we move,
Heads bowed, spirits broken,
Circling wider and wider, eccentric, untrue,
Trying to attune ourselves to finest strings,
But ah, failing, failing.

W. B. Yeats (1865- 1939), Irish poet, wrote *The Second Coming.*

FOR THE CIVIL RIGHTS ASSASSINATED

They were permeable,
Malleable, pliant.
They were soft
For the bullet entry.
But see what an unfair advantage
They had over the murderous foe.
They had no bombs or guns,
But steadfastly defended themselves
With the blazing color of righteousness,
Which can endure everything.

Martin Luther King Jr. (1929-1968)
Malcolm X (1925-1965)
Medgar Evers (1925-1963)
Et alia..........

SPIRIT AND FLESH

The Spirit willing, flesh is weak.
I think it written wrong.
Except for His horrific night
When grief was dark and strong.

But that was then and far away
And never had occurred
To many who proclaim today
That flesh is now the Word.

LONG AGO BIRTHDAY

In the beginning of that day
You came to our bed.
We laughed and played,
Had breakfast of cereal and milk.
You were your natural self,
As predictable as ever the whole day through:
A few hard licks and tears,
Amazement at new things, all old,
New seductions that did not fail.
Grandmother came over for cake
And we opened some presents for you.
She left, your mother and I quarreled.
It was a Sunday, and you were two.

SNOWBIRD

I am old
And I am not sober
But I remember
The Championship Game
When I was alone
Under the basket
And the long pass came
And I turned and placed
As gently as a baby
The ball on the glass
And it rolled
And rolled
And fell off the rim
Just as the buzzer
Shot this crushing pain
Through every part
Of my body and brain.

MARTIN HEIDEGGER SPEAKS

"I seek universals.
There is something of a difference
Between a word and its meaning.
We have theology and philosophy, yes,
But we must have more—
Something foundational.
Every discipline is only divergent thoughts
Needing a convergence."
So Heidegger and his misguided disciples
Daily took their spades
And toiled and scraped and dug,
Seeking through their anxiety,
The facts, only the facts,
Cold, subliminal, and brutish.
There are none.

Martin Heidegger (1889-1976), German philosopher, wrote *Being and Time*.

PASTORAL CALL: SCHIZOPHRENIA

Thomas has been on the front lines in five World Wars.
It was Hell.
Today he said there were thousands of ships
Coming here daily, from all over the world.
He had to check to see where they were from,
Where they were going.
He said this used to be the world's loveliest farm
Till it went wild at the beginning of time.
His wife, he declared, never loved anyone
But her very best friends.
She did not have an enemy in the world.
He has been in care for thirty-five years,
All the wires crossed forever.
Who was Thomas? Where has he gone?

FREEDOM RIDERS

Their sign read,
"For Freedom We Will Die."
Some
would love that.
You know it, but
What else do you have to give?
You show one way to change it all.
Another is to pridefully watch your beautiful daughters
Become Homecoming Queens
In "their" South.
Grindingly, such history will play out.

Freedom Riders, an important event in late '60s Civil Rights Movement.

SUPERMAN RECOVERS

I fall to my knees and retch.
I lurch, I gag, I foam.
My senses spin and eyes roll in this throbbing skull.
Vision is blurred and knees are weak.
They are ingenious in their methods
And I wonder when and where
And what is next.
Never mind.
I am faster than they are fast
And am now miles away from them and danger.
There is good to do and I am good.
This, another episode, another futile attempt,
And I have won!
But still I rise and think how close they came.
I survive another brush with kryptonite.

ARMISTICE DAY, 1918

I scan the red horizon;
The sun is rising fast.
A war-torn world awakens,
Is this the day at last
When we lay down our weapons
To look, embrace in love,
Is this a cataclysmic
Arousal from Above?
No evidence forthcoming
To dream such airy dreams,
I aim my gun awaiting
More sad, fantastic schemes.

Hundreds of combatants were killed on November 11, 1918, in the
hours before Armistice.

SERENGETI

Dark is the time of lions,
And the stalking and killing of
Zebras and wildebeests.
As heat waves rise and tremble
The stripes of still zebras
Merge into background trees.
The foolish wildebeests run.

JAMES BALDWIN LEAVES AMERICA

I

I am dead.
I was a white man,
Now a suicide among thousands.
Middle-aged, I had not achieved
The "American Dream."
I grasped and fought.
Caught nothing; touched nothing.
I ended it alone, in my swirling anomie.
Durkheim would understand.

II

I am not dead.
I am an African-American
Who *heard* about the "Dream,"
But never dreamed it.
For it would not come true,
Could not come true
In that oppressive racial morass.
So, I live on, in France.
I work, I toil
Day by day.
My time will simply come
At the end.
Before then, from the Bottom,
I strive.

James Baldwin (1924-1987), African-American writer. Emile Durkheim (1858-1917), French sociologist, wrote *Suicide*.

JOHN 4

Jesus came stumbling through quivering air.
His dry tongue, a thick rope,
He leaned against the well posts
And in one motion turned to sit.
But the rocks were too hot,
And he stepped back in with a start.
"I had no idea it was such a distance.
I hope they find some food.
And here comes a brazen Samaritan
With an empty jar,
And even emptier life.
O Father, give me strength.
What Messiahs have to go through!"

ABUSED ADOLESCENT

Having father come at you
With a kitchen knife
Is an indelicate situation
Handled by strategically juxtaposing
A dinette chair between,
And pushing until he bounces off
The jamb, and falls sobbing
Onto the linoleum floor.
At thirteen, the heart is clean,
Without a scratch or trickle of blood,
And high and boasting.
But older, the drunk father gone,
The heart is cut and broken,
And the mind, like he lunged
For the mind, and struck swiftly,
Time after time after time.
His precise, surgical description
Well matches the deep I simply cannot see.

MAN AGAINST THE MOLE

I had not imagined you so sinister,
So nightmarish in appearance.
But I have tracked you down at last,
And aided by my Terrier, I shoveled you out.
I drove him away to look you over,
And I flipped you to the walk.
My yard reminds me of weightlifter arms,
Rippled and puffed up.
But now you are mine, captive,
Out of your deep, dark element.
There is a whole mythology of moles,
And you must surely die.
I can give you to my dog
Or to the heel of this thick boot.
I stare you in the "eyes,"
Repent,
And let you live.

ON NOT USING WORDS

"I told you twice without the words
But you refused to see
That both of us are better off
If both of us are free."

"I think it always best to put
The painful thing in words,
Than look back on the yesterdays
And never then be heard."

But he could not accept the fact
She would not choose to wait,
And that the two would never be,
Despite a nuptial date.

So was the time, ten times ago,
And now a wiser man,
He rues that judgment of his heart
And goes as best he can.

CHRISTINA'S DAY

after Andrew Wyeth

Afternoons bored her to tears.
The passive mother lived in dramas
Of daytime television,
Acting out in the space of that dull brain
All she would never be allowed outside.
The sultry Summer pained most,
The dampness of perspiration, grit,
Stagnant air, all oppressed,
But never moved mother
Who rocked in the dank parlor,
Breathing the odor of mildew
Grown too familiar with in all those years.
So far from town, up the stairs,
Door closed, Christina could only feel alive
Lying in bed, fan swirling,
Holding the thin, rough world
Perfectly in place.
Her mother knew.

Andrew Wyeth (1917-2009), American visual artist, painted
Christina's World.

MANDELA ENTERS ROBBEN PRISON

Off shore, on the beautiful island,
Prison guards speak Afrikaans, not Xhosa.
They greet with snarls, clenched fists,
And for years you must be "Boy," or "Kaffir."
Here, you will lose your mother, a son,
And Winnie will go off a different way.
Out there, she believes violence is solution.
You do not, in here or out there,
Though it frequently crosses your caged mind
With each demeaning debasement.
These soldiers of Apartheid will respect you
Only when they lose their grip,
Are mortally afraid,
And realize it is all quite over.
They will then come for you,
Give you power,
As the whole world watches
To see if amazing South Africa
Can right itself
To join the dysfunctional "Family of Nations."
You did your best,
The land struggles on,
And in death you are enrolled in the annals
Of true greatness, forevermore.

Nelson Mandela (1918-2013). First President of South Africa.
Winnie Mandela (1936-218), Nelson's second wife.

NORMANDY

The wind whips across the sand.
From one side the beach stretches,
Unaffected, undulated.
A man could jump from ridge to ridge
Till he reached the water.
From the other side it angles
Affected, level
Into its North Sea mouth.
Today, but not every day,
There is unusual flotsam on the shore.
There has been a vicious fight:
Planes raced, mortars belched,
Bullets screamed, rockets flashed,
Soldiers scurried across this beach,
Soldiers fell to their knees and died.
Now heavy bodies quietly impose
Their figures in swirling, stinging sand.
Around them sandpipers dart and peck,
But nothing else moves save arms and legs
Of those who almost reached land's end.
It has been a glorious day!
Men have been brave.
They have shot others at close range,
Struggled hand to hand,
Run bayonets through foreigners like themselves.
It was victory. It was defeat.
The beach is secure, contested no more.
Soldiers move on.
As these lie here in cold, wet silence,
Our minds step around, beside, across them.
What they have given to this ever-shifting sand!

From us, the temporary, fragmentary earth
Preserves only the shallow imprint of our weeping feet.

The Allies invaded Northern France on June 6, 1944.

KAY KYSER GIVES UP MUSIC FOR CHRISTIAN SCIENCE

What else could I do?
As I
Was thinking
It occurred
To me
That I
Was also
Being thought!

Kay Kyser (1905-1985). American bandleader who retired from music and became a Christian Science practitioner.

EPILEPSY

I try to imagine what it would be like
Having an uncontrollable seizure disorder.
I try to imagine walking normally, doing normal things,
Then suddenly being flung down with such force
That no wonder it was once thought
To be the work of demons.
In ages past you *might* have been revered,
Possessed by gods, blessed.
Now your condition is given to new medicine,
Or a temporal lobe resection.
Once I viewed an autopsy,
Witnessed the skull sawed
To reveal a large gray brain.
I was amazed at the maze of intersecting networks,
The delicacy of it all.
The autopsy was of a beautiful sixteen year old boy,
With severe epilepsy, verbally unable to tell how sick he was.
He died from pneumonia.
No gods involved.

WIRE HAIR FOX TERRIER

In the next room,
He is howling and barking
At the hard rain with thunder.
I remember exactly
How he got this unfortunate fear.
During another bad Summer storm,
I was away.
You, too, were afraid, and clutched him, a small puppy.
He has been like this since then.
See how you affect things?
I should have been there.
I am not afraid of these storms.
You could have held me.

EUCHARIST AS ENEMY

I

And so I cannot please you at this table.
You knocked, I did not.
The meal was plain, bread and wine.
You blessed it.
The conversation was warm,
I sensed your concern for things,
Animals, and persons I did not know.
After eating we walked and returned to rest.
But you have changed.
Something has gone out of you.
A stranger sits where you sat,
With rough scowl and punishing eyes.
How can I tolerate such a one
Who sits, only sits,
Demanding and repeating,
"This is not a Holy Communion world!"

II

Father John of Kronstadt, it is said,
Would shout and argue with God
During his ministration of the Divine Liturgy.

Saint John of Kronstadt (1829-1909), protopresbyter and Synod
member of the Russian Orthodox Church.

SNOW WALK

I left one sunny morning
With no real place to go.
The temperature was falling.
I took no thought of snow.

But as I blithely wandered
The sky began to gray.
Yet, I enjoyed the turning
Of Winter's restless day.

When flakes began to flutter,
I turned to realize
That I had lost my bearing
Under now frightful skies.

Since then I wander daily
To find where I have been,
But think it does not matter—
The snow and I begin.

JOHN CLARE

Thinking of conflicts within myself
I am reminded that I started off with violence and
My parents' divorce
And ended up working for years
In a State Psychiatric Hospital
Which reminded me of John Clare
Who in his youth helped built an "insane asylum"
And died there as a patient in old age
The difference being that
I did not have much of a childhood
And that I went there just in time
To tear down something
I had been building in my head
For a long time
And I think that I got out of there
Just in time.
The beautiful John did not.

John Clare (1793-1864), English poet.

GRACIOUSNESS IN HIGH PLACES

One of the most gracious acts
I have ever heard about
Was when a group of Boy Scouts
Had dinner with the state's Governor,
And one of the special guests
Turned over a glass of water,
And you how embarrassed and ashamed
He must have been.
But then the Governor reached for something
A bit too brusquely
And knocked over his water, too.
He laughed and said,
"Boy, we're clumsy, aren't we?"
Which loosened things up quite considerably
I am sure.

THE DIVINE HOUND

after Francis Thompson

Down, down the dismal days
When a drooling moon and
Fainting stars kept heaven's rabbit
Running, running.

Thought through on frosty morn
Of resolution: turn, turn,
But windy beach saw the same hare
Running, running.

Toward thin ice, early trod
Feeling crisp, icy, but there no word.
Turn, turn, running, running
Heaven's prey faster.

Stained glass brought thoughts of "Yes!"
Glosses there were made in tears,
But souls do not swing on those arms,
And still running.

Then, where moon--star—ice found
Torn muscles, clipped nerves,
By a sacred Tree breathing Wind,
Waiting, waiting, LIGHT!

Francis Thompson (1859-1907) English poet, wrote *The Hound of Heaven.*
Psalm 139: 7: "Whither shall I flee from Thy presence? Whither shall I go from Thy Spirit?"

ON COURTING MARY AFTER EASTER

Your husband, a fine carpenter, I hear.
The son was a sensation in his day.
Jerusalem still speaks of him, I fear.
Was he of us, or did he go astray?

No matter. I am here for other things.
My wife was taken from me, as you know.
A fever which our Summer season brings
Unmercifully doomed her months ago.

I say too much! I should not carry on,
Except remind that we have both known pain.
You have no one besides your youngest, John.
I crave the joys of hearth and home again.

I leave, but please consider what I say,
And send me word as soon as you are able.
Pray on it as you eat this raw, first day.
Some wine and broken bread are on your table.

After Acts, chapter 1, Mary literally disappears from the pages of
the New Testament.

HE DID NOT GET THERE WITH US

When Martin stood with Moses
On the frightening, deadly mountain,
He did not see the rape, carnage, and plunder
Of advancing Israelites.
He saw a Promised Land of lions and lambs,
Loving embraces, mercy, equity, and peace.
Moses could not come down,
Died in the gentle arms of God,
And was buried in that remote and barren waste.
Martin did come down to the earthiest of things,
A strike by exploited Sanitation Workers.
On that last night he powerfully repeated
His unchanging, passionate message:
He told Power to "Do the right thing!"
And he walked away.
Later, at the Lorraine Motel,
Finality erupted in plain sight
As the 30.06 easily felled him
Onto the crowded concrete balcony.
He did not get there with us,
But he had preached as strongly as anyone ever
What *shall* ultimately prevail
In the plodding, drawn-out, unpunctual Kairos:
The hated, despised, rejected, bloody, battered, cross-borne
Triumphant Justice of the Lord God Almighty.

Inspired by the last sermon of Martin Luther King, Jr. April 3,
1968. Kairos is God's time.

POPULATION AND ETERNITY

Still the children do not stop.
There will be no bread for them.
But Jesus says, "Suffer them to come."
In his arms they will be
As lights shining in the firmament.
The final age of life eternal
Is forever shouting to the world,
"Be fruitful and multiply!"
Against its cry
There is no logic, no contraceptive, no ethic,
Nothing but selfish economics of the faithless.
And so, they *will* suffer.

COUP D'ETAT

With formidable speed comes the specter of the night.
In soft and silken shadows descends the mist,
The incorporeal stealing courage from courage.
An icy veil of shade extends velvet fingers
From tree to tree and heart to heart.
Eerie silence behind the shade
Covers the earth in gloom.
Spirits rise from sunken graves
And glide across thin vapors.
The frightened sun retreats and slowly dies
To the gray, the grayer, the black.
Silently, stealthily, completely,
Night lifts a slender arm as King.

AT SHRINERS HOSPITAL

Hobbling along, crutches in grip,
The slightest inclines a pitfall,
Never wondering, never doubting,
Never asking very legitimate questions.
He has faith, some faith,
Some kind of faith in God, Jesus, Holy Ghost.
Never doubting any of it.
I doubt.
I question,
Who was never a moment crippled in my life.
My illness and suffering came
Only through my eyes, and there, deep,
I have long, lonely nights
Clutched and grasped in sweat and tears,
For, trembling, my simple crutch.

STANDOFF

I saw it for myself:
A child who resisted everything
Her parent tried to do.
There she was, cute as a button,
Standing in diapers,
Hands on hips,
Fiery eyes,
Aggressing mother to tears
With her new-found sphincter muscles.
Control may be a future issue.

THE MATCH ON THE TIP OF THE TONGUE

Deliciously sadistic,
She places match in the curl of her tongue,
And sets on fire more than she knows.
Winking once, she smiles,
Inviting self punishment
In odder, cooler ways.
This is not for me, I protest,
Even as her finger turns
From straight, back to the sensuous mouth.
I watch in wonder,
High School boy at carnival, sideshow, red light.
She amazes further with erudition
Quite, quite beyond belief:
"Hercules," she coos,
"Did not grow old."
Embarrassingly new to such myth and metaphor,
I age defenselessly
Into the hot, moist, sultry Summer night.
I *should* not be here.

RWANDAN MACHETES

The muscular arm goes up and down, up and down.
The road is hot and dry, but soon slick and sticky.
"We are Hutus, and no Tutsi will rule us.
This we must do, but in doing it we are kind enough.
We are quick.
Better this than death by a thousand cuts.
And as Black on Black, no one will care,
Or try to stop us."
In the end, chair-sitters will appear
To conduct a passionate political autopsy,
Then write a limp, flaccid report
For the spineless United Nations.
But from April through July, 1994,
There were no "victimless crimes,"
And stacks of lifeless men, women, and children
Would argue that point, passionately
As Presidents, Kings, and Prime Ministers
Enjoyed exotic cocktails, smiling insipidly
While holding up a shiny, glittering ball,
Saying, "Look at this. Look over here."

The Rwandan Massacre left close to a million dead, millions in exile. Hutus and Tutsis are still not on favorable terms.

WHERE HE KISSED HER

In the room where he kissed her
Sat an old woman
At a round table drinking Claret.
He had been there before
And he knew the woman,
Full of learning and insight,
But unwilling to talk to anyone
Except the few old men who came by
From time to time.
She could have told them the romance
Would not last, and that the heated love
Would soon cool to embers.
She could have told them both,
But she sat mute
Observing the kiss and their flushed faces
Whose hearts beat as one,
Not knowing they would soon enough
Be in other places
Not remembering the old lady
Or her intelligent eyes which spoke volumes,
But did not say a word
In that dark room with a dying fire
And an old woman quietly drinking
Her rich wisdom.

NOT KNOWING

Not knowing what to make of it
I made nothing at all.
That careless recklessness began
My long and tragic fall.

Like trees misreading weather signs
To bloom what cannot last,
I reinvent my memories
And cling to what is past.

BEST FRIEND

The dog on the arm of the chair
Awaits the young Master's return,
Not knowing he will not appear,
For cancer has taken his turn.

And so through the long days and nights,
This faithfulness on sad display,
Not knowing the Master has found
New friends who are eager to play.

EULOGY FOR THE MEN OF HADDAM

after Wallace Stevens

Let us not impugn the thin men of Haddam!
To accuse them of gross indifference
Or gold-mongering is one thing,
Partly true, as young women assert,
But it is quite another to portray them
As ethereal, gaunt, mystical,
As superstitious and crude.
They shall not be branded
By the stuffy men of Hartford.
Unfair!
They must not, at this late date,
Be relegated by the stroke of a pen
To a place of surrealism
In the netherworld of time.

We are obliged to redeem them,
To reassess their role and place.
It is true they have despoiled nature and women.
That is part of their history,
Undenied by the truly great men of Haddam.
But who can forget the heroes of that lineage?
Proud, good men who stood
For justice and mercy and peace.
Can we allow to wane the names
Of those who gave so much and asked so little?
Time and eternity will honor the likes
Of Antonio, Bertold, and George---
Should they not?
And who could ever rest,
Contemplating for one moment

That he would be forgotten
Who fathered so infinitely much:
Here, I speak, of course, of Adam.
Let us not, let us never
Assail the men of Haddam.
Rather, let us place eternal golden blackbirds
Around their venerable, unpoetic feet!

Wallace Stevens, (1879-1955), American poet, wrote *13 Ways of Looking at a Blackbird*, in which he referenced, "O thin men of Haddam……" Haddam, a city in Connecticut. Stevens lived in Hartford.

SIC TRANSIT GLORIA MUNDI

Perhaps only a slave
Could speak such truth to power.
Standing behind the hero, holding a golden crown,
Whispering, "All glory is fleeting,"
He could get away with such daring talk.
But few rulers listened,
And the King would simply shoo away
The chariot chattel to perform other
More menial, but less fraudulent tasks.
The scheming would continue, with dramatic plans
To spread the flower-strewn, fleeting glory
Across unnecessary, blood-soaked fields of battle,
Hoping for another decadent display of fawning *populi.*

"All glory is fleeting," a favorite maxim of Roman Stoics, including
Emperor Marcus Aurelius, (121 CE-180 CE).

REINTERPRETING SOME THINGS

A few hours ago
I spent some memories
In Southside Virginia
Where I saw a man and a woman fighting
And in childhood rage I wanted them
Out of my life forever
But I came back
To realize again that something else
Had arranged all that
They were gone
And would never be going
Into that sad ring again.

TWO RESERVATIONS

On any given day in Pine Ridge Reservation
Sixty percent of resident Native Americans
Have neither electricity nor running water.
Life expectancy for males remains 48.
I also know that just blocks
From the most affluent enclaves
I can find razor wire
And if I linger past dark
Can hear distant gunshots
Lilt through the chill air.
They cannot, however, distract
From 30 year old Scotch in Baccarat glasses
Accompanied by extra large Cuban cigars.
Those gates shut tight
And big-armed security guards rarely shoot,
But are always sharp-eyed on Ready.
They rule the world.
Deep in the womb of the frigid Wyoming night,
The Res continues in unrelenting, invisible despair.

DISCHARGE

When he ran into her arms,
She closed her joyful, streaming eyes.
He did not, but looked skyward
Where a wisp of cloud
Crossed a blazing sun.
It was not a glad-to-see-you moment
But one where the sentence was completed,
The legal price paid.
In her arms he was not at all sure
That they were enough to keep him
From the audacious scheme
Suggested by the sadistic lifer
When he was in another embrace,
His cold, calculating eyes squeezed shut.

YAKS

I know a few things about yaks:
They are tough,
Can survive thin Himalayan air,
Wolves are a huge problem
And will tear the throats of the lambs,
So they are easy to pen
And generally tame enough.
They are highly prized by Tajiks
For scores of reasons.
The Soviets named a warplane
After this indomitable, shaggy beast.
It was a very good choice.
They cannot fly
But seems likely yaks are here to stay.

BLOOD DIAMONDS

De Beers will always buy it,
But not from you, a black man,
From a middleman, white Afrikaaner.
How do you hide it, then,
For you found it in the hard, red mud.
No one was watching, so you hid it
Deep in your jaw.
You kept it from the slavers
Who would shoot you dead
If there was any suspicion at all.
Back in the tattered tent
You wonder what to do, where to run.
But the choice is easy,
And you do what all the others have done:
Wrap it in a filthy piece of rag,
Bury it in the ground,
And dream about it.
You will get up tomorrow
And shovel in the hard, watery muck,
Full of unimaginable riches
And spent bullets shot into real men
Who found and kept what the masters
Called their own.
The stone from your jaw may be
Discovered by the next expendable man
Or who himself may find a beauty
Only to be hidden away,
Perhaps to be found, buried again,
Or lost forever.
This is your quiet, unarmed rebellion.
This is your heartbreaking, woeful Africa.

Blood Diamonds: stones discovered through essentially slave labor.

FCL: FUTURE CHURCH LEADERS

Just one more step and I be
A bonafide Ph.D.
Another doctor for His nation!
But, o dear, the dissertation.

I guess I could investigate
Why Jesus looks so underweight
In every picture I have seen.
My, was that party-goer lean!

And I have thought that I should wonder
What God has to do with thunder.
I confess my lone suggestion
Is eternal indigestion.

Or then again I could inquire
Into the Spirit's breathing fire.
I do suspect a chain from gnosis
To some form of halitosis.

I said I wanted to find out
What Conversion was all about.
But, gee, that sounds a bit too rich.
I think that I was wise to switch.

I really wanted to compose
My work on "Ancient Swimming Clothes,"
But *Dissertation Abstracts* said
That was in someone else's head.

O me! I picture it all now!
Just waiting there I'll gently bow
And take my stand for all to see:
A bulwark of theology!

With men like me around to teach,
And men like me around to preach
There is no problem I can see
For Jesus' Christianity.

But now which topic shall I claim
To make my humble rise to fame?
Just one more step and I will be
A bona fide Ph.D.

FOR AUDEN

I love you for Kierkegaard.
I love you for Old English.
I love you for helping us laugh
In the face of great tragedy.
You were a superb combination
Of things I appreciate most.
Thank you for finally coming around,
For the prayers, Offices, and all.
You were a few days here, a few days there,
Recognizing the traveler in us,
The not-being-at-home in the heart.
In your travels you came my way.
You read your poems: they were alive.
I was impressed; I was confused.
Sometime later you passed away.
I heard myself repeating: "Stop all the clocks…."

W. H. Auden (1907-1973), English poet. Last line from his poem
with that title.

AFTER THOMAS MERTON

I had believed that monasteries
Would wall out vulnerability and temptation,
Then reflected that throughout his life
Jesus remained completely open to both.
Wise, worldly Merton had intoned
That when you enter a monastery
You take yourself with you.
Merton was with Merton a very long time.

Thomas Merton (1915-1958), American Trappist monk and writer.

STROKES

I step into the ward and am overwhelmed again.
I must proclaim their healing!
I announce the recovery of rhythm,
Smooth ambulating, skipping, running,
For these limp, dragging limbs.
This serves absolutely no purpose.
It is a violent surd,
Fitting no theology or anthropology.
If this heresy, I am a heretic.
God takes no delight in strokes.
The rocks and these drab walls shout:
"They must be whole."
And I declare their healing!
I close the door behind me.
I have survived.
My Defense Mechanisms were strong, once more.

CITY THOUGHTS AT EVENING

after William Collins

Early, early form the dewdrops,
Lowly, low the cow bell rings.
Quickly, quickly jump the late birds.
One by one they fold bright wings.

Often I have seen this evening.
Oftener I've dreamed its fall
When my heart was in the hustle
Of a teeming city mall.

There among the brushing shoulders
Of the impersonal town
I have seen its beauty clearest,
I have heard its sounds surround.

Stopping in such peaceful moments
Raptured by my heart's delight
I have seen the passers staring,
Puzzled by so strange a sight.

Do they never have such visions?
Do they never dream such dreams?
While I make my hectic journey
I find solace in such scenes.

William Collins (1721-1759), English poet, wrote *Ode to Evening*.

THE ANGEL'S FAREWELL TO THE HOLY MOTHER

Dear Mary, Mary, not contrary,
Placid, docile, sweet, demure.
Are these the words you want to say?
They drip, are unctuous, but so pure.
I say you can protest it if you choose.
I think that it will happen anyway.
You are a simple handmaid of the Lord,
But when I leave please know the die is cast.
And, no, I cannot say just how or when,
But you will understand it when you should.
I leave you to this painful isolation.
I can't come back to reassure or calm.
Interpret slowly, child, this visitation,
Do not succumb to panic or alarm,
And bless the strange One in your tender womb.

COMMAND TO POETS

The land is always new
Like war trenches which give way
To an Eden and to a God
Who tells all poets
To rediscover the power of words
And like Adam
To name again the wondrous things they see.

EASTER POEMS

I

See how they come
Eyeless in Gaza,
Flinging their impotence at the Christ
Who is not here.
Away. Away.

II

Back, back I go through Winter trees
To the source of my aching back's mind.
In Spring the heart unfolds like a lily.
In Spring these terminal woods grow thick.

III

O Christ, I crave your peace.
In this chair of my disjunct existence
I seek a wholeness.
It is only from you.
Pledge me a point at which
My divergent passions unite.
Draw me forward to the mark
Extracting what displeases you most.
Give the elemental education
To produce what you would have me become.
I crave your peace.
I am ready.
Send purifying fire,
And may my residue hear you say,
"Welcome, blessed child. You are home."

The verses in this volume attempt a poetic analysis and interpretation of highly diverse topics. They do not shy away from violence, tragedy, and loss, but also include more tender, humane subjects, like parenting, romantic love, wonder, and amazement. They subtly posit that all of life is overseen by a benevolent Deity, who though often unrecognized, dispenses grace to all.